INNOVATION IN RUSSIAN SCHOOLS

Edited by
Z.I. Batioukova and
T.D. Shaposhnikova

Translated by
Maria Korolov

Phi Delta Kappa
International Studies in Education

We can only see in a picture what our experience permits us to see.

Edgar Dale

The Phi Delta Kappa International Studies in Education Series was established as a way to enlarge the common experience of education by publishing studies that bring to readers knowledge of heretofore unfamiliar theories, philosophies, and practices in the profession of education.

As the interdependence of nations becomes increasingly evident and necessary with the passage of time, so too must our understandings about education become shared property. In thus sharing, we come increasingly to comprehend one another across civilizations and cultures, for education is at the core of human endeavor. Through education we pass on to succeeding generations not merely the accumulated wisdom of our past but the vision and means to create the future.

Innovation in Russian Schools is the third monograph in this series.

Previous titles:
Elementary Teacher Education in Korea
Teacher Education in the People's Republic of China

INTERNATIONAL STUDIES
IN EDUCATION

INNOVATION
IN RUSSIAN
SCHOOLS

Edited by
Z.I. Batioukova and
T.D. Shaposhnikova

Translated by
Maria Korolov

PHI DELTA KAPPA
EDUCATIONAL FOUNDATION
Bloomington, Indiana
U.S.A.

Cover design by
Peg Caudell

Library of Congress Catalog Card Number 97-65264
ISBN 0-87367-494-0
Copyright © 1997 by the Phi Delta Kappa Educational Foundation
Bloomington, Indiana U.S.A.

PREFACE

This book is the second product of a collaborative effort by the Russian Academy of Education, the Moscow Education Department, and Phi Delta Kappa International. That collaboration first resulted in a book that was published in Russian in 1995 by the Russian Academy of Education under the title, *The School of Tomorrow Is Born Today: The Experience of Innovation in Russian and American Schools*. That book included several articles by Russian educators, seven of which compose this volume, and several articles by American educators, which were reprinted from the *Phi Delta Kappan* journal. Eli Weinerman, a graduate student at Indiana University, provided abstracts in Russian of the American articles for this Russian publication. The American articles, which are not reprinted in this volume, are listed below for reference. Maria Korolov, a Russian-American journalist, writer, and editor, translated the Russian articles for this volume. Korolov is the former national editor of the *Moscow Tribune*.

The authors of the articles in this book are practicing teachers and researchers. They present their experiences of innovative solutions to school problems and suggest possibilities for the development of the modern school in post-Communist Russia. They discuss the management of the schools and the education environment in general, the development of students' personalities, and the growth of students' knowledge and abilities in various disciplines.

American readers will likely find that several of the articles are quite different in tone, style, and content from typical education articles by American, Canadian, or other English-speaking writers. This is partly, though not wholly, an effect of translation, as an attempt was made to retain as authentic a Russian voice as possible. However, it also should be recognized that education writing takes on a style and form in Russia that is, indeed, substantively different from comparable writing in the United States.

Educators and students of education with an interest in comparative studies will find these articles both informative and interesting, not merely to compare Russian education to education systems elsewhere, but also to witness the evolution of Russian education as that nation undergoes profound internal changes in the nature of the state and its relationship with its people.

Donovan R. Walling
Editor of Special Publications
Phi Delta Kappa Educational Foundation

* * *

The following articles by American educators were included in the original Russian publication:

Amenda, Robert. "What's Happening in Horizon High School?" *Phi Delta Kappan* 64 (November 1982): 204-205.

Banks, James A. "Multiethnic Education and the Quest for Equality." *Phi Delta Kappan* 64 (April 1983): 582-85.

Barnhardt, Ray, and Barnhardt, Carol. "Chipping Away at Rural School Problems: The Alaskan Experience with Educational Technology." *Phi Delta Kappan* 65 (December 1983): 274-78.

Edwards, June. "To Teach Responsibility, Bring Back the Dalton Plan." *Phi Delta Kappan* 72 (January 1991): 398-401.

Harmon, Saundra Bryn. "Teaming: A Concept that Works." *Phi Delta Kappan* 64 (January 1983): 366-67.

Lickona, Thomas. "Four Strategies for Fostering Character Development in Children." *Phi Delta Kappan* 69 (February 1988): 419-23.

Lotto, Linda S. "The Unfinished Agenda: Report from the National Commission on Secondary Vocational Education." *Phi Delta Kappan* 66 (April 1985): 568-73.

Mikulecky, Larry. "National Adult Literacy and Lifelong Learning Goals." *Phi Delta Kappan* 72 (December 1990): 304-309.

Walberg, Herbert J. "Productive Teaching and Instruction: Assessing the Knowledge Base." *Phi Delta Kappan* 71 (February 1990): 470-78.

Watson, Bruce. "The Wired Classroom: American Education Goes On-Line." *Phi Delta Kappan* 72 (October 1990): 109-12.

TABLE OF CONTENTS

INTRODUCTION

Russia is undergoing the most difficult ethical, moral, political, and economic period of its existence. The moral and political pendulum is briefly frozen at the bottom of the arc. Where will it swing next? Will it return to a frightening totalitarian past of a dictatorship or will it start, slowly and with difficulty, to build positive momentum toward a society free from fear and from governmental lies — toward a future of well-being.

The greatest hope of the Russian people is the development, the moral and ethical healing and rebirth, of the schools. The Russian school has chosen its path to a humanistic, democratic society. But will the school have the ability and the conditions for the realization of these aspirations? We believe that it will. And the proof of this is the book that you hold in your hands.

In this book we present the experiences of Russian pedagogues, both practicing teachers and researchers, and of scientific researchers in the area of innovation and reform. We would like to express our immense gratitude to the authors who have shared these articles with us. They well understand that moral support of these aspirations is very necessary. They share their experiences of innovation with Russian and American colleagues.

The acceleration of scientific and social progress and the critical economic, ecological, demographic, political, and other world-changing events that have taken place in recent years — all of these inevitably are reflected in the education system and in the contradictions and difficulties of bringing up and teaching children.

Purely traditional forms, methods, and means of education do not meet current demands. Nor are unchanging curricula and pedagogy adequate to meet the needs of a changed, and changing, society. People, both as objects and subjects of educational activity, experience the new socioeconomic, ecological, regional, and global changes faster than we educators can keep up by changing the content and the process of education.

Understanding the new in education and disseminating leading-edge educational techniques and theoretical thought are problems of education reform. But attempts must be made, and that is the nature of this book. The essays included in this work examine the processes and events that characterize the new education environment in Russia. They show how problems that arise are variously approached, in different contexts, in the educational practices of modern Russia.

We very much hope that this international exchange of ideas will be continued. American colleagues who visit Russia can see firsthand that everything that they read about in this book actually exists in Russia. We look forward to ongoing cooperation with our American colleagues.

We dedicate this book to those who work in the field of education, to those who study it and those who practice it, and to those who create public education.

Z.I. Batioukova, head scientist
T.D. Shaposhnikova, senior scientist
Institute of Theoretical Pedagogy and
    International Education Research,
Russian Academy of Education

REMEDIAL EDUCATION IN THE ISMAILOVO EDUCATION COMPLEX

N.G. Avdeichuk

N.G. Avdeichuk received her education in the Moscow Pedagogic University, specializing in primary education. Her research field is innovative reforms of teaching practices. She spent the last five years studying the education problems of at-risk children. In the Ismailovo socioeducational complex, she is developing a model of remedial education with special emphasis on the emotional development of children.

Remedial education is a relatively new phenomenon in Russian public schools. It serves to provide psychological and educational support for children with actual or potential difficulties in learning and socialization.

For a long time, Russian schools have been structured around a single goal, that of educating the average child. This situation has led to large numbers of children being alienated from the school system, children who, as a result of biological, social, or psychological factors, could not fit into the narrow constraints of the "standard student." Annual statistics show a notable increase in the degree of maladaptation to school, and ever-larger numbers of children have been identified as belonging to the group considered to be educationally at risk. Today, every fifth student entering school cannot adapt to the traditional educational process.

Worldwide, scientists continue to search for effective means of helping children in the at-risk categories. Research in this field is being conducted in Russian schools as well. Five years ago, our teaching faculty joined in the testing of the remedial education model.

The socioeducational complex at Ismailovo was founded in 1989. The necessity for its creation was dictated by the circumstances that arose at that time in the East Ismailovo district. At the end of the 1980s, apartment buildings targeted at young families became popular. Hundreds of these young families flooded our district. Simultaneously with the families came nursery schools and kindergartens. On the basis of existing Middle School #716 and these new construction projects, a new socioeducational complex began to be built. Should we continue with the traditional system of education (kindergarten, primary school, middle school) with all its problems of continuity, or should we create a new social institution of continuous education and guidance? The law allowed us to model a new type of education system, which could become the social and educational center of the district.

During the past five years we have been working on creating this socioeducational complex. The biggest challenges that we see facing us are the development of an effective system of socialization, the creation of the optimal conditions for self-expression and growth of the individual personality, the identification of abilities, the formation of humanistic opinions and creative thinking skills, and equipping students with a base of knowledge about nature, society, and the individual at work.

In order to meet these challenges, we are developing a unified program of guidance and education, which includes both regular school and preschool. The central concerns about the family and the student are faced by the Center of Early Childhood Development. Children two and three years of age and their parents work with teachers, a pediatrician, and a psychologist. Children between three and six years of age go to the kindergarten, which opened three years ago. Young children who are reared at home may attend the Center of Aesthetic Development and study music, art, choreography, and athletics with experienced teachers. Children also meet their future instructors here.

Today we work according to developmental, adaptational, games-oriented, and traditional systems of education. Parents can choose their child's education program when the child enters the primary school. In middle school the students themselves choose their program and, together with a diploma, they can receive a certificate attesting that they are qualified to work as a camp counselor, tour guide, or computer operator.

The socioeducational complex is an integrated education institution where some 2,000 students of various abilities learn and receive guidance. The movement to mainstream children with learning difficulties, as much as is possible, into public schools is a characteristic of the education culture in many countries of the world. "As little as possible external variation and as much as possible internal differentiation" is the founding principle of today's progressive school. Having tackled the problem of teaching all students enrolled in the complex, we had to create a system of educational assistance for those who had difficulties.

Our first steps served to put to use the experience of Russian and foreign schools. Forging ties with education research institutions became a necessary part of our program. Research groups headed by Dr. G.F. Kumarina and Dr. S.A. Belicheva of the Ministry of Health, Division of Childhood Hygiene, helped us to develop a system of supplementary education that took into account the makeup of the student body and the resources available at the complex.

Education systems are some of the most complex of social systems, where all elements combine to work toward a common goal. The goal of a system of supplementary education is to create the optimal conditions for the socialization and education of at-risk children in accordance with their individual needs and potentials. The two determining elements of this system (the goal and the composition of the student body) required that all links in the education chain be re-evaluated. The teaching and administrative staff needed to be reorganized; the techniques of supplementary education needed to be developed for all age levels; new methods of guidance needed to be created; new equipment and materials needed to be found; and we needed to forge ties with the outside world.

The Diagnostic and Correctional Center of the Complex

Who can and should work with children who are educationally at risk? In answering this question, we decided that the first quality a teacher must have is sympathy, or willingness and readiness to come to the aid of the child. Not all teachers can maintain their patience and goodwill while making progress at a snail's pace. A problematic child can work only in conditions of full moral and material support.

In deciding the answer to the second question, who should work with children's problems, we started with the goals of the system of supplemental education. Of course, the central figure of the system was, and remains, the teacher. However, experts in learning disabilities must also be included: speech therapists (virtually all children with learning difficulties suffer inadequate speech development) and special education teachers (in an integrated system cases of retarded psychological development are inevitable, as are instances of learning disabilities). Psychologists also work closely with these experts and with teachers. And the participation of doctors — pediatricians and psychiatrists — is essential.

In this way, a focal point appeared in our school's supplementary education system, centered on the diagnosis of children's learning problems, the correction of identified developmental inadequacies, and the cooperation between the school and the parents. In our complex, this was titled the Diagnostic and Correctional Center (DCC). Today, the DCC serves children in the district ranging from five to 15 years of age. For 2,000 children, in addition to teachers, the center also provides five psychologists, four speech therapists, one special education teacher, and one psychiatrist.

Preschool

The great teacher, Yan Amos Kamenskii, once said:

> The nature of all creatures is such that they are most flexible and can most easily be molded while still young. Once they age, they are no longer amenable to influence. Soft wax can be shaped into any form; but once it hardens, it crumbles instead.

These words, first uttered in the 17th century, are still relevant today. Modern research in the field of supplementary education shows that prevention and correction of problems are both best begun at an early age, long before the child enters school.

Tests conducted in 1989 of the readiness for school of 189 seven-year-olds demonstrated the following:

- 96 children belonged to the 2-3 group*;
- One child was an invalid;
- 12 children were socially disadvantaged;
- 29 children had learning difficulties;
- 42 children suffered from phonetic or phonematic speech defects; and
- 27 children had mildly expressed speech disabilities.

Because of this testing, we could determine the preventive and remedial steps necessary in working with preschool children.

Thomas Weiss, in studying problems of at-risk children, wrote that a guiding principle of working with such children needs to be "kindness"; with school-age children, "beauty"; and with adolescents, "truth." Therefore, we determined that the basis of preschool education must be the inculcation of a relationship based on kindness toward nature and people. In addition, we developed a program of special individualized and group-based remedial classes. The preschool program included special speech development exercises, practiced by the entire group (of 20 students) with the teacher. The speech therapist works with the more difficult students to improve enunciation, to develop an ear for sounds, to increase vocabulary, to discourse on a given theme, and to converse in a social setting. Children especially enjoy activities in the Fairy Tale Room, where each child can act out the role of a favorite fairy tale character. This room also is a good setting for children to create their own fairy stories and tall tales.

Then, during the Riddle Hour, children learn to develop logical thinking skills. Adults and children alike make up the riddles. After all, the world is full of mysteries! Those children who find this activity difficult work with a special education teacher. Day after day of steady work brings positive results — though these results are not always easily quantifiable.

The preschool education program is rounded out with music, art, dance, and theater. Besides the traditional program, required

---

*"2-3 group" is the Russian designation for children with multiple, nondebilitating physical handicaps.

by the government, qualified teachers also work with the children to help them produce their own creative works. It is impossible to overestimate the influence of art on the child's development. Each art form has its own specific effect. For example, it has been noted that children who do not know how to sing have difficulty learning to read and that those who have trouble drawing are also slow to talk and write. Consequently, music, dance, art, and theater teachers work with the development specialists of the Diagnostic and Correctional Center.

The music program is centered on singing, playing simple musical instruments (spoons, whistles, and rattles), improvisation, and moving to music. A great deal of attention is paid to teaching children to hone their hearing and listening skills. Some students, those having particular difficulty, spend additional time practicing rhythms.

The young children also work with clay. While learning the folk traditions of the Moscow region, they make clay toys, just as their great-great-grandmothers and grandfathers once did. They mold the material, first hesitantly then with increasing assurance, into little beads, coins, birds, horses, and so on. After the clay pieces are fired and painted, they are turned into very attractive toys and figurines, which the students give as gifts to friends and relatives, show at exhibitions, or use to decorate their homes.

Finally, with the help of a speech therapist and a psychologist, the children's theater gives students the chance to test their dramatic talents. Through theater, children develop their speaking skills, practice memorization, and begin to shed behavioral problems. With the help of characters out of literature, the children turn into familiar figures and learn to interact with adults and with peers.

Physical education also plays an important role in the development of the child. The favorite activity of our students is swimming. Each day, our preschool's swimming pool fills with their joyful voices. By six years of age, most children are learning to swim. In addition to swimming, preschoolers are introduced to competitive sports and gymnastics. For students who are interested, or who have been referred by the Diagnostic and Correctional Center, we also offer Hatha Yoga and U Shu.

As I mentioned previously, primary school teachers are introduced to their future students a year in advance. The first meetings take place in kindergarten a year before they enter first grade. In reading together, playing, or taking a walk in the park, the teachers and students become better acquainted.

At six years of age, if the parents so desire, those students ready for formal education can enter the first grade of the four-year primary school. Those students who are not yet ready for school, or whose parents prefer to keep them in kindergarten for another year, enter the preparatory group; and the program continues with an expanded menu of activities and workshops.

Our method of ensuring continuity between primary school and preschool already has produced positive results. First-graders easily and quickly adapt to school, while the integration of the education and the developmental programs has allowed us to intensify the learning experience. The active inclusion of families in the process of developing education programs and early intervention have allowed us to reduce the number of children in the at-risk categories over the four years of the program.

Following is a chart that compares the number of students at-risk in 1989 to those in 1993 in three major types of groups:

At-Risk Group by Type of Student

Student type	1989	1993
Total number of students	189	197
2-3 group	51% (96 children)	50% (98)
socially disadvantaged	6% (11)	3% (6)
learning disadvantaged	15% (28)	11% (22)
Not at risk	28% (54)	36% (71)

The introduction of the system of supplementary education in the preschool environment has led to a decrease in the number of children in the socially disadvantaged and learning disadvantaged at-risk categories. Early detection of problems and goal-oriented work with the children has allowed us to overcome or eliminate developmental inadequacies. In addition, our diagnostic capabilities allow us to develop a curriculum for this first stage of the educational process.

Primary School

The basic principle of education for the beginning primary student is *beauty*: the beauty of nature, of people and of human thought, the beauty of relationships, and the beauty of things that people make.

All fields of activity begun in kindergarten continue in the primary grades. At the time students enter first grade, the Diagnostic and Correctional Center is aware of the readiness to learn of 8 students out of 10. During the spring months, the center tests all children new to the complex both individually and in groups. Information about the size and the structure of the at-risk group is necessary in order to adequately adapt the education process for the entering students.

In traditional Russian schools a system of tracking for remedial education is prevalent, and remedial classes for children lagging in educational development run parallel to mainstream classes. After evaluating the pluses and minuses of this model, we decided to create an integrated system in which teachers are able to offer necessary psychological and educational support without disturbing the unity and cohesion of the entire class.

Today we have a set of remedial classes and integrated supplementary education classes. With the parents' permission, children who demonstrate difficulty learning are assigned to the special diagnostic class, numbering 9 to 13 students. All first-graders have the option of attending regular school. By the end of the first grade the only children left in the diagnostic class are those diagnosed with delayed mental development. Their further education is structured around a program of progressive integration. During the first half of the day, children attend their special class; and during the second half they participate in workshops and other activities together with the general student body. During the next three years, as children master the remedial materials, they are transferred to the traditional classes.

In addition, we also have the integrated program of supplementary education. A mixed but significant group of students have single, definite developmental problems. These students join the general classes, while the individual subject they have difficulty with is taught by a special education teacher. For example, our school has special groups studying grammar and Russian, mathematics, and physical education. In all other subjects the students are taught in common. In addition to working with small groups, we also use individualized tutoring (again, in accordance with the results of our diagnostic program). The special education sessions are not an addition to the general education program but are an integral part, and so time is freed up for the child to pursue other academic and related interests.

The curriculum of the primary grades, for all classes, includes several mandatory subjects: Russian and reading, mathematics, earth science, music, art, physical education, and industrial education. In addition, our school also offers logic (for the first and second grades), information science (for third and fourth grades), and English or German beginning at second grade. Ethics is taught to all students from first through fourth grades and, beginning with fourth grade, Russian history is taught. Extracurricular remedial workshops include speech therapy, in which children with difficulty communicating participate in group seminars on social interaction.

We also maintain a relaxation room, which is open throughout the day for the use of students. Here, psychologists work individually with students to relieve negative emotions and restore a positive attitude.

During the second half of the day, children choose between clubs, art studios, and wood shop. After classes, students can explore their talents in art, music, and handcrafting. The library occupies a very important place in the school. A comfortable reading area, shelves well-stocked with children's literature, a games collection and — most important — a supportive librarian attract large numbers of students daily. In remedial education, also, the library plays an important role. Reading is the leading learning skill, the major means of receiving information. Children who are introduced to the world of books also become aware of the richness of human knowledge. The school library helps all students, even those with learning difficulties, to become dedicated readers.

During the three or four years of primary school we are thus able, with our refined system of supplementary and remedial education, to solve the basic developmental and education challenges of this age group: to motivate students to learn, to lay down basic knowledge and academic skills, and to instill a humane relationship to nature, people, and their work. The diagnostic center enables a program of social adaptation for all students and helps to optimize the educational condition of each student.

During middle school the system of remedial education is just starting to gain strength. There are still challenges to be faced, such as the question of the educational status of those graduates who have finished the remedial education program and the task of preparing children from the at-risk groups for a profession. Psychological services play a crucial role in middle school, with accurate diagnosis and resolution of behavioral and other problems a necessity for the adolescent student. We have only just started working on these problems in our complex, but some results are already apparent, demonstrating that we are on the right track. For example, there are no instances of willful absence from class or involvement with the police among any of the students in our supplementary education classes. And, as a result of cooperation between the school and the family to involve students in positive educational activities, there have been no cases of adolescents dropping out of school or running away from home.

The External Environment

If we are to talk about the overall influence of the school system on the educational environment in our district, then the activity of our remedial education system must extend beyond the boundaries of the school. During the past five years, we have attempted to establish connections with cultural and medical institutions in the community, as well as with the police and justice systems.

Our closest neighbors are the MZhK cable television station, the Theater of Mimicry and Gesture, the Lavrenev Public Library, the Child and Adolescent Health Center, and the local police station. Of all of these institutions, the television station probably is the most influential. Children spend a great deal of their time in front of the television set. How can the blue screen stop being the enemy and become an ally? Working cooperatively with the television station, we have developed programs for children and adults. A daily program, "Our Home," informs viewers about interesting events that take place in the community and in school and introduces that evening's showing of the featured movie. The program, "In the Wardrobe," is about and for children.

With the help of television, we also hold parent assemblies, in which we introduce specialists from our complex. Parents can call in by telephone and ask questions. Putting television to good use, specialists of our Diagnostic and Correctional Center meet and talk with adults about children's problems and how to resolve them, and about new methods of addressing specific developmental difficulties. Television also presents a means of optimizing the educational process. Regular videotaping at the request of the center allows the center's staff to better judge the effectiveness of instructional methods, to receive additional information, to watch results in a dynamic setting, and to generalize work experience.

The Child and Adolescent Health Center has allowed the complex to treat children with more complicated health problems. We are actively using the sanitarium method of treating weakened children; many students receive physical therapy; and students also have access to psychotherapy.

Our proximity to two theaters has affected the direction of the aesthetic education of our students. Students enjoy not just watching plays and shows but also participating in creating dramatic presentations.

Beginning with the second grade, children studying in our school become readers at the Lavrenev Public Library. Beginning with the children's room and later expanding to the foreign literature, music literature, Russian literature, and scientific and popular literature collections, children broaden their intellectual horizons and expand their worldview. It is not an accident that some classes are taught in the library.

Working with at-risk children, we also have established contact with the juvenile division of the local police department. School personnel and police officials work together to identify troubled families and to intervene early with at-risk children.

The system of supplementary and remedial education is one of the fastest-developing sectors of the modern public school. The results we have achieved after four years of work with at-risk children have demonstrated that we have chosen the right road. By sharing knowledge with our Russian and foreign colleagues, we have been able to enrich our own programs, because others also have helped us to solve problems dealing with the organization and administration of our complex.

We would be very happy to receive feedback from the readers of this article about our experience working with at-risk children. Our address is Ismailovo Education Complex, Pervomaiskaya Ulitsa, d. 111, Moscow 105203, Russia.

THE SCHOOL AS THE FOUNDATION IN A SYSTEM OF LIFELONG LEARNING

S.V. Gorbun
and
O.K. Tikhonova

For several years, Preobrazhenskaya School #1690 in Moscow has been working as an Educational Advising Complex, joining together several education institutions including a kindergarten, a grade school, and a vocational school. The complex was conceived and implemented by the creative endeavors of the school's faculty, headed by school director S.V. Gorbun and his deputy, O.K. Tikhonova.

The teaching faculty of Moscow School #1690 has conducted research over a period of time in order to establish and develop a new education and guidance complex, now called Preobrazhen-skaya (Transformation) School #1690. This research drew from educational experiences in a variety of schools (gymnasia, lycées, specialized academies, and other socioeducational and educational and guidance complexes) in the city of Moscow and other regions of Russia.

School #1690 has been in existence for more than 26 years. During this quarter century, it has accumulated a great deal of experience in educating children between the ages of six and 17, in teaching more than two dozen academic subjects beginning with grammar and ending with trigonometry, and in organizing a system of supplementary education through a number of study groups, studios, sport clubs, expeditions, and field trips. However, the times constantly demand further innovation. Therefore, the teaching faculty of the school is always in search of new, more effective methods, means, and forms of education and guidance.

Today's society makes new demands of school graduates, of educational content, and of the organization of the education and guidance process. The social context of education as a whole is rapidly changing, and the old schools cannot face the new challenges without fundamental restructuring. In a time of great instability the school must, first of all, serve a defensive function. This is not to say that schools should protect their charges from the problems of modern life. Rather, the task must be to prepare students for a difficult and ever-changing socioeconomic and political situation. The democratization process in Russia has torn down the strict centralized education system, which was monolithic in concept, in curricula, and in textbooks. Differentiation is the new reality of education in today's Russia.

In analyzing the fundamental characteristics of the current education environment, the teaching faculty of the school concluded that it is necessary not simply to improve on the existing framework, but to create a qualitatively new structure based on a differentiated approach, the development of democratic relations, and continuous education. Such a structure, in our opinion, could be an education and advising complex (EAC) that would include several crucial components, including kindergarten, primary and secondary schools, and colleges and universities. Teachers thus face three crucial challenges:

- To create, in an EAC system, a center for preschool education (CPE) for the early identification of abilities and talents in children aged four to six years.
- To develop unified education programs — in other words, methodical approaches to content, forms, and methods in education and guidance — all along the kindergarten-school-college chain in order to ensure continuity of education.
- To participate in a program of childhood development through a cooperative effort between physicians and psychologists at the complex, which would ensure the maximum fulfillment of psychological, physical, and intellectual potential and needs of the individual child.

An EAC structure allows for a many-sided and multi-leveled system of education. Therefore, in order to implement this EAC structure, we produced the Preobrazhenskaya School #1690 — or Transformation School — by uniting with a former kindergarten (#111) and Preobrazhenskaya School #374 in Moscow. We should note that this structure is not cast in stone and could change and improve as a result of further work. The components of the EAC, now Preobrazhenskaya School #1690, are displayed in the accompanying table.

THE EDUCATIONAL ADVISING COMPLEX #1690		
Preobrazhenskaya School, City of Moscow		
Preschool	3-6 years	System of early education that builds on and includes the results of international and Russian experience (M. Montessori, L.V. Zankov, D.B. Elkonin, V.V. Davydov, Wegner) First classes of primary school
Primary School	6-9 years grades 1-4	Classes of developmental education General education classes Remedial education classes
Middle School	10-12 years grades 5-7	General education classes Remedial education classes Enriched classes
	13-15 years grades 8-9	Humanities class Physics and mathematics class Polytechnic class Vocational school Technical colleges
High School	16-17 years grades 10-11	Humanities class Physics and mathematics class Natural sciences class Colleges and universities

Primary School

Primary education is one of the most important parts of the general system of education. It is specifically in this stage of development that children learn basic knowledge, skills, and academic habits and develop the ability to think logically. The speech, will power, and the feelings of the child all develop during this stage.

Currently children enter the first grade at six or seven years of age, depending on their psychological and physical development and degree of preparation for school. In the first grade, the child inevitably encounters difficulties: incompatibilities between preschool education and the demands of new teachers, inadequate development of speech, memory, spatial awareness, arm musculature, and so on. In spite of all efforts, difficult situations can arise and the child's adaptation may be hampered.

In order to overcome these problems, preparatory programs have been created, in which children aged four to six years meet twice a week to study music, English, and art and use games to get ready for formal schooling. They learn to analyze the sounds of words, become familiar with counting, and develop spatial awareness, logical thinking skills, and speech (vocabulary).

The experiences in the Center for Preschool Education help children to better adapt to school and to begin learning successfully once they enter first grade. In fact, the sessions at the CPE are led by teachers who will later work with the children in primary school. Thus each child gets to know the teacher, which eases the transition to formal school.

In the first stage of formal schooling, the primary grades, special attention is paid to developing the character of the program. Classes of intensive education according to the L.V. Zankov system operate simultaneously with classes in which education takes place according to the government program.

The classes built on the L.V. Zankov system have been in existence now for two years. The transition to this didactic system forced us, the teachers, to strive toward ensuring that the student entering school not only is taught facts, skills, and habits but also develops other aspects of his individuality. The contents, didactic principles, and forms and methods of this system allow us to teach in such a way that children do not lose enthusiasm for learning, and negative emotions do not arise. In class, questions are constantly posed, arguments flare up, and children learn to defend their opinions using evidence. The classes are conducted at a high level of difficulty and at a fast pace.

Students can exercise their right to receive an education that satisfies their interests, needs, abilities, and potential — if a multi-level, many-sided approach to education is implemented. The organization of such an approach is a difficult, involved process that demands the analysis of the psychological, intellectual, and physical development of the child up to the point of graduation from primary school.

At the end of the third grade, the students are tested by psychologists working in our EAC. The tests serve to identify the level of the intellectual development of the child and the inherent (or acquired during education) predispositions of the child to the study of the soft or hard sciences, the liberal arts, or technical work.

Final testing at the end of primary school, stressing verbal and mathematical skills, is used along with the observations of teachers and the conclusions and recommendations of psychologists to allow us to separate the soon-to-be fifth-graders into groups. As a result of this process, we are able to identify students not yet ready for middle school. For this group of children, we open an equalizing class (of educational support) so that the students can master materials not sufficiently absorbed during the fourth grade.

Middle School

In the transition to middle school education, many students suffer a drop in academic performance because it is hard for them to adapt and fulfill the requirements of subject area specialists. (In primary school, the major academic subjects are all taught by one teacher.) Therefore, in order to reduce the psychological stress on students and to ensure educational continuity and adjustment of requirements, joint seminars of primary and middle school teachers are organized. Furthermore, teachers who will work with the children in middle school visit primary school classes and observe the children. In this way, fifth-grade classes are formed according to the ability levels of the students.

It is necessary to meet one more challenge: to help the students identify their talents and to interest them in some specific subject. With this end in mind, we have instituted a system of clubs for fifth- and sixth-graders. These clubs are organized around major potential interests: mathematics, literature, biology, foreign languages, technology, and the service trades. All students are required to participate in a club, and club meetings are part of a student's class schedule. During the course of an academic year, students can change clubs. Club activities are structured so as to allow for a cyclical learning program to facilitate such changes.

In middle school, starting at age 12 or 13, children begin to determine that their talents and interests lie in certain disciplines.

At this stage, in the eighth-grade, the class schedule begins to include departmental classes. It is understood that, no matter how hard we try with clubs, clubs do not allow for a whole class period to be spent investigating the technical or humanitarian sciences. Nor can a whole class period be spent practicing vocational skills. For these reasons, departmental classes are scheduled during either the first or last period of the day in order for students, who otherwise study all subjects in common, to separate into groups to pursue their specific interests.

Again, some problems arise. Departmental classes can be effective only if the following conditions are met:

1. The group of participating students does not exceed 10 to 12 individuals.
2. The students who join a departmental class not only are interested in the subject, but also have sufficient preparation.
3. The time spent in departmental classes increases the knowledge base or the specific skills required by the discipline.

Of course, not all participants have the inclination or the ability to pursue intellectual endeavors. A large number of eighth-grade students prefer practical subjects. Our EAC is equipped to teach students woodworking, metal shop, sewing, macramé, and cooking. Likewise, part of the student body does not intend to continue education past middle school. The goal of the EAC is to help them to acquire a trade. To this end, a vocational school (Education and Manufacturing Facility) plays an important role. Through a cooperative agreement, we can teach students such skills as typing, stenography, business correspondence, auto repair, and computer use.

By age 15, many teenagers are aware that they must either begin to prepare for college or to receive vocational training. Students wishing to enter the tenth grade of the EAC must past competitive entrance exams. Those students who finish the ninth grade of the EAC with grades of "A" and "B" ("5" and "4" in the Russian system) and who have letters of recommendation are not required to take the tests.

High School

What should be taught in the 10th and 11th grades? How can the EAC help students prepare for college?

Colleges and universities can be arbitrarily divided into the technical colleges, liberal arts colleges, and those oriented toward the natural sciences. From the experience of previous years, one can say that most students in our EAC are interested in preparing for the technical and liberal arts colleges.

Preparing for the Technical Colleges. In our EAC, students can continue their education and prepare for entrance to technical colleges. We have signed an agreement of cooperation with Russian Technical Institutes, an organization that allows us to have our classes in physics and mathematics taught by college professors.

As a guarantee of adequate education we have the professors themselves, who have not only taught for many years at a college level but who have also served on entrance committees of colleges and universities. They are very familiar with the requirements of the entrance exams and ably combine covering the mandated national curriculum with preparation for these exams. The final exams of this program are simultaneously entrance exams for institutes and universities working cooperatively with Russian Technical Institutes. These courses not only provide a deep and thorough knowledge of the subject material, but they prepare students very well for their further studies.

As the time spent on physics and mathematics increases, the time spent studying other subjects is reduced to a minimum. The literature requirement is reworked and aimed toward preparing the students to pass the college entrance exam. Similarly, the English language curriculum also is revised. The classes use texts that feature technical subjects, and students spend more time translating texts and studying grammar, which will help them work with technical literature.

The largest drawback of this program is that the preparation in physics and mathematics is only partially funded by the school, with the bulk of the costs being defrayed by the parents. Russia is suffering from hyperinflation, and the cost of the classes (as set by Russian Technical Institutes) constantly increases, often at a rate outpacing the wage increases of the parents. This situation forces us to look for other sources of funding (such as from outside sponsors) or to develop a new relationship with colleges and universities, at a lower cost to ourselves. We also would like to expand the program beyond the fundamentals into additional courses, allowing students to study more narrow technical subjects.

Preparing for the Liberal Arts Colleges. Parallel to our technical preparation program is the liberal arts program. This program also is made necessary by the interests and talents of the students.

Those students who are especially gifted in the area of the humanities are, as a rule, at odds with the more technical subjects. In the humanities sequence, technical subjects are reduced to a minimum and students spend more time studying literature, history, languages, philosophy, and rhetoric. This allows these students to develop their artistic potential and to find their own place in life. In the end, society reaps the benefits of its new teachers, historians, writers, artists, and so on.

In creating this sequence we met with a number of challenges, including curriculum development. We developed curricula for Russian literature, foreign literature, history of Moscow, English, rhetoric, and moral philosophy. We also increased the number of hours that students spent studying literature, history, and languages. And we introduced new subjects, even as the number of hours spent on technical subjects remained the same. As a result, some students were severely overburdened, which was reflected in how much they were able to learn.

At one time, studies in the humanitarian class were combined with attendance at lectures in a school of economics, but we are rethinking this strategy and probably will discontinue it.

Similarly, we have noted that entrance requirements need to be tightened. Mediocre students simply cannot handle the volume of work that is required.

Conclusion

As this is written, our work continues. Teachers and administrators are developing new curricula, instructional methods, and materials, such as textbooks, for the expansion of the system of developing education from the primary school into the middle school.

Within a year, students from the developing education classes will leave primary school and enter middle school and subject teachers must be prepared to continue the work. This is a difficult task for teachers who have spent many years working under the old system. In order for the program to be successful, they must, first of all, want to change their style of teaching, to become enthused by the idea of developmental education and to be steeped in it. Only then will they understand the basic principles on which this system is based, the principles that determine the methods and techniques used in teaching. With this goal in mind, and under the guidance of an expert psychologist, the teachers will spend a year studying and attending seminars. A great deal of help is offered by the teachers of the primary school, who already have mastered the skills needed to work under the system of L.V. Zankov.

Visiting colleagues' classrooms and watching and analyzing videotaped lessons taught at other schools allow us to work fruitfully toward this end. We continue individual work with teachers and researchers, synthesizing our accumulated experience.

The new school has now been in existence for more than two years. Only an amiable and cooperative group of like-minded individuals, headed by forceful administrators, could have overcome the difficulties we faced and learned to find joy in small triumphs. There is, then, scope for the abilities of both the faculty and the administration of the school.

CREATING READING TEXTBOOKS FOR THE PRIMARY GRADES

R.N. Buneev
and
E.V. Buneeva

R.N. Buneev is chair of the Russian Language for Foreigners Department of the humanities school of the Automotive Academy. He is the author of research articles about the problems that foreign students have learning language analysis skills. He also is the author of Russian language textbooks.

E.V. Buneeva is an assistant professor in the Department of Russian Language Methodology at the Government Education University. She studies speech development in primary school students and the teaching of text-based reading during classes in Russian language and literature.

Picture a child bent over a book, reading eagerly and often — a child who cannot be torn away from a book, who prefers reading to watching cartoons or playing videogames. For some parents, this is a familiar sight. But for many, it is an unattainable dream.

Is there anything that can be done so that children will love and want to read? How can their interest in and love of reading be stimulated? At first, we could only ask ourselves these questions. Then we tried to answer them. Our answer is that it is vital to start with the textbooks, namely, the very first textbooks, those written for the primary grades.

Reading is a traditional subject in Russian primary schools. Reading education is centered on special textbooks — readers — in which poems and prose compositions are grouped thematically and are accompanied by questions and exercises. The themes vary, from fairy tales to works by Russian and foreign writers, stories about nature and animals at different times of the year, the world of work, and others. During the Soviet period a great deal of space was occupied by stories with a very definite political and ideological message, which served a deliberate social purpose: the formation of a "communist worldview." As a rule, these stories were heavy-handed and were selected not because of their literary or humane merit, but because they were in line with certain political and ideological standards. For this reason many wonderful, truly literary examples of children's literature had no place in the readers. This could not but affect children's interest in reading. Moreover, other problems also arose.

First, nine-year-old children, leaving primary school and entering middle school, often experienced serious difficulty reading works of literature even when they were capable readers. They could not grasp the depth of meaning of a text, to sense and judge the special qualities of a literary work, the beauty and the expressiveness of the author's words. Second, not all children loved reading or wanted to read, were interested in the process of reading itself, or could orient themselves in modern children's literature. Third, the majority of children did not possess to a satisfactory degree the skills necessary to understand fully what they have read. In other words, the acquisition of these skills was not the major goal of their early reading classes.

Today's traditional readers are largely antiquated in content; and attempts to partially revise them are, in our opinion, unwarranted. We need conceptually new textbooks, textbooks that can serve current needs. It is obvious that a large part of today's society has rejected the totalitarian regime's system of morality, wherein society was placed above the individual and an idea was more important than human life. We are now beginning to move to a new morality, centered on the individual. And we are beginning to understand that a human life is worth more than a principle or an idea and that family, love, and human relationships are more important than problems of production.

All of the concerns mentioned above have led us to attempt to create a new set of readers that are qualitatively different from those that existed earlier. To explain that difference, we first must look at the goals we aim for in teaching reading to children between six and nine years of age. These goals are to teach children to read literature, to prepare them for systematic study of literature in middle school, and to instill the fundamentals of reading so that the child is well versed in reading and comprehension skills — in other words, is capable of reading independently. In order to meet these goals, it is necessary to overcome a number of challenges:

- To awaken the child's interest in reading and, on the basis of this interest, to lay down the skills and habits of reading;

- To show children that literature is an art form based on words and to teach them to pay special attention to words when reading literary works;
- To develop the students' spoken and written language skills and their creative abilities; and
- To lead young readers through the doorway of literature into the world of human relations and moral values and to mold their cognitive identities.

In 1992 and 1993 our reader series, *Free Minds*, was published in Moscow. This series includes the first-grade reader, *Sundrops*; the second-grade reader, *Small Door into a Large World*, in two parts; the third-grade reader, *Once Upon a Happy Childhood*, in two parts; and the fourth-grade reader, *In the Ocean of the World*, also in two parts.* The manuscripts received grant support from the Soros Fund for General Education in the Humanities, and the books were recommended by the Russian Education Ministry for use in public schools.

What are the distinguishing characteristics of these books? First of all, we offer a certain system of child-oriented reading. All of these textbooks share thematic elements and are united by an internal logic. That is, first-graders read poems and small stories by modern Russian writers about toys and games, about friends, parents, and children, about animals and nature. Through literature, they learn about themselves and the world around them.

In the second grade, the world that children discover for themselves through these readers widens. The reader includes folktales from the peoples of Russia and other countries (stories, riddles, folk songs) as well as short stories. In reading these texts, the children enter a "common spiritual space" and understand that the world is gigantic and multifaceted yet still a single whole. No matter when people lived, it is obvious that they always valued hard work, patriotism, intelligence and kindness, courage and dignity, passion and faithfulness. Qualities such as laziness, greed, incom-

---

*Translator's note: "In the ocean of the world" also can be translated as "in an ocean of light" because *world* and *light* are the same word in Russian.

petence, cowardice, and meanness were universally despised. To demonstrate this, *Small Door into a Large World* includes folktales that have similar titles, common themes, or the same main idea.

Thus in the first and second grades, children are introduced to two of the most interesting sources of children's reading material: modern children's literature and folklore. In third grade they discover for themselves the world of literature in all its variety and read not only fairy tales and children's literature but also the so-called adult literature: poetry and prose not specifically written for children but that are close to and understandable by children. *Once Upon a Happy Childhood* includes classics of Russian and foreign children's literature, works by Russian writers and poets of the 20th century accessible to children, and works by modern children's writers.

In fourth grade children receive a unified presentation of the history of Russian literature, about writers and their heroes, about themes and genres. We attempted to create a course of Russian children's literature of the 18th through 20th centuries for reading classes. In the book, *In the Ocean of the World*, the texts are arranged chronologically so that children can gain a preliminary understanding of the history of literature as a process, of the connection between the content of a work and the time in which it was written and with the author and his or her life, and of the relation between concrete historical concerns and eternal human values.

The selections in *In the Ocean of the World*, as well as the series of included questions and exercises, help the children to repeat and systematize all that they have read earlier. Such is the internal logic of the series of children's readers during the four years of primary school.

The second qualitative distinction of our readers is that, in addition to the traditional thematic principle, we also build the books around other principles. We use a variety of genres, build a sense of the author as a creative individual, draw connections between children's and "adult" literature, present literary works in their entirety, and consider the thematic or artistic relevance of any given piece to the children before we include it.

For example, throughout the *Free Minds* reader series, we present works from various genres: short stories, excerpts from novelettes, folktales and authored fairy tales, lyrical and narrative poetry, songs, counting rhymes, riddles, and miniatures. During the four years of primary education children frequently read different works by the same authors, written for children of various ages and distinct in theme and genre.

Thus children are gradually able to form a complete understanding of the writer's art, to draw a picture of the author as a creative individual. It also is vitally important to us that the readers must be relevant to the children. They should be about the children themselves and about what is interesting and important to the children. The works that the children read are connected to their tastes and needs. This approach is a reflection of the principle of artistic relevance.

In realizing this principle we have also attempted to motivate the children to read. Why should I read these very texts in this exact order? What if I want to read selectively? Can I switch around parts of the book? The answers to these questions we give in a slightly unusual form, and this is yet another unique characteristic of our books. We have introduced common characters that we have invented ourselves that allow us to build each book (and, therefore, the sequence of reading lessons) in the form of a heuristic conversation.

A rabbit called Poos is the hero of the book, *Sundrops*. He turns into a boy named Peter Zaitsev (Rabbit) and goes to first grade. Peter hardly knows anything at all, and other first-graders help him. They read poems and stories together with him, explain the hard parts, and answer his questions — that is, they assume the role of the teacher, which is, of course, the best way to understand the subject. Because there is a person who cannot understand the simplest things, the children learn not only to read but also to clearly explain and to discuss. In this way, manners also are motivated (Peter reads poems about proper behavior), and the sequence of readings becomes a natural one. Our hero and his friends learn about the world. The questions also become an integral part of the text: "How would you explain this to Peter?", "Help Peter and explain. . . ," and so on.

In *Small Door into a Large World* there are other heroes — second-grader Sasha and a fairy-tale character, a small *domovoi* named Afanasy.* Afanasy loves and knows fairy tales. Together with Sasha, they travel through the stories; and Sasha asks a large number of questions. Afanasy answers them or helps Sasha find the answers himself. He talks about books, recites merry poems, and poses riddles. The dialogues between Sasha and Afanasy connect the texts and motivate questions and exercises related to the texts. The entire second-grade reader is an interesting game, a trip into fairy-tale land.

In the third-grade reader the sequence of sections and of the texts within each section are linked with the natural flow of the life of the family of a girl named Anastasia. Anastasia is a third-grader and reads *Once Upon a Happy Childhood* together with her father. The dialogues between Anastasia and her father are the thematic links between the texts. In addition, the dialogues contain a great deal of additional information about writers, books, and life in general.

In the fourth-grade reader, *In the Ocean of the World*, the introductions to the texts are in the form of dialogues between two children and a literature professor. With the help of a modern time machine, they travel into the past, into the pages of history of Russian children's literature and not only visit the past but also meet "live" writers, sometimes even speaking with them. In addition to the texts of literary works, this reader includes comprehensive supplementary materials, such as biographies of the writers and excerpts from the memoirs of their contemporaries, from letters, and from diaries.

All of the readers are illustrated with original drawings by a group of young talented artists. During the compilation of the books, we used traditional accompanying illustrations for the

---

*Translator's note: A *domovoi* is a character out of Russian folktales. He is a small creature who lives in a house and helps keep it warm and cozy.

texts, photographs, and "children's" artwork. The characters that tie the books together also are constantly present on the pages of the readers. All of this makes it possible to organize the texts in an interesting way. These, too, are distinctive characteristics of the *Free Minds* series.

Together with the readers, we also have prepared a teachers' guide for primary school reading classes that outlines our conception of the project. In various sections of the guide we cover the themes of the reading material and the parameters of the reading methodology. We list techniques to improve reading comprehension, which are gradually introduced in the lessons. An example of such a technique is looking at the title of a piece. Students learn to examine the meaning of the title and its connection to the contents and main idea of the text. They take a hand in making up alternate titles, guessing what the text will be about based on the title, noticing the illustrations linked to the key words, and so on. Other techniques include determining the meaning of a word based on context; making up subtitles for parts of the text; creating simple and complicated outlines; answering questions about the text before reading, while reading the text, and after finishing the text; forming new questions while reading (a kind of "dialogue with the author"); and determining the main idea of the text.

With our series of readers, we introduce children to a large set of concepts: poetry, prose, oral storytelling traditions and their genres, theme and main idea, characters and the ways they are created, short stories, plays, comparisons, metaphor, poetic epithet, and so on. Our readers also allow for developing writing skills alongside reading abilities, some literary analysis of the texts, and the observation of authors' language and style.

Many schools in Moscow and other Russian cities have been using our books during the past two years. Based on our observations from visiting classes and talking with teachers, children, and parents, we can say that many children have developed an interest in reading books and in their reading classes. We have seen evidence in many children of a desire to read works in their entirety that they had read only excerpts from in class. Children have begun to visit the library more often and to ask their parents to buy them books. Teachers have noted a marked increase in the speed at which children read and in their vocabularies, and they have been pleased to find many opportunities that the texts provided to work with dictionaries and to expand children's worldviews. Our books have been used successfully both in public schools and in special advanced schools because they allow teachers to be creative in the teaching process.

Many times we have had the opportunity to observe as teachers use our books with great interest and enthusiasm and as students actively and eagerly express their opinions about what they have read and attempt to explain their ideas and their understanding of the text. During the reading process the students form their individualities — intellectually, creatively. And they become free minds.

MODELING EFFECTIVE INSTRUCTIONAL PROCESSES

A.A. Ryvkin

A.A. Ryvkin is the director of Ismailovo, the largest education complex in Moscow. He spends his time wrestling with the problems of administering the large-scale complex and providing leadership in developing effective instructional processes.

For the past 15 years I have been visiting the teachers of my school, and recently I have been visiting other schools as a government monitor. The same kind of work is carried out by my colleagues all across the country. During the course of my wandering, I have become more and more disappointed by what I see in classes. Often, my impression of the education environment can be summarized as follows: The teacher comes to class having a certain idea about what he (or she) plans to teach to the children that day. After the teacher conveys this information, he demands that the students repeat it back and then evaluates what he hears.

The majority of teachers will insist that the desired instructional goals have been achieved, that an understanding of the information was firmly planted in the minds of the children. Furthermore, these teachers — it seems — are convinced that the information they convey in class is the absolute truth, and that this information is the continuation of a series of preceding truths.

This teaching method cannot truly educate a child. I am not saying that this method does not have a place. In fact, in those subjects where the child learns how to receive information (reading, writing, mathematics), this method may even dominate. I am saddened, however, by the fact that 99% of all teachers work by this method, regardless of subject, whether they are middle school or primary school teachers.

Fortunately, another method has begun to appear. The classes taught by this latter method can be summarized as follows: The teacher, with a certain idea of the information he plans to convey, "packages" it (in the form of text, video sequence, picture, game, and so on) for the lesson and offers the students the opportunity to experience it and relate to it in their own ways. Of course, the students must be prepared with ways to gain knowledge (meaning that they can read, write, and are competent in basic mathematical skills). Then the teacher organizes communication among the students in order to ensure that all students understand the "package" and its inclusion into the existing knowledge base.

The "packages" vary, depending on the abilities of the students; but general discussion can be carried out with the entire group. This solves a basic problem of education: the integration of individual and group learning and the collective-frontal teaching method. By using this innovative method, all children can learn, which solves yet another problem — the social adaptation of the child.

This is an innovative teaching method that has been kept out of the schools for a long time because government monitors did not understand the principles underlying the method, and they considered it to be too involved and abstruse. It did not fit well into their conception of the educational process. Indeed, there is a natural corollary that the majority of those teachers who are able to organize such an instructional process, at least intuitively, also possess self-knowledge or self-awareness.

This relationship is critical. Thus it is important to look into the "laboratory" where this instructional process is prepared. Here, we see the specifics. The teacher who prepares to teach a traditional lesson is in the role of the teacher-as-translator. Everything from the content of the lesson (what to teach) to the methodology (how to teach) he receives in the form of a curriculum, lesson plans, and an accompanying teacher's guide. The teacher does not face the problem of how to teach, because the daily evaluation of the teaching process is easy to carry out with a limited number of tools. Everything is simple. Children reproduce what they are assigned, grades are received and written down, and everything goes according to plan. But when final exam time comes, the results do not correspond to those preliminary evaluations.

How can this happen if the teaching was adequate? Why, the guilty party is obvious — the child. The child did not want to study; he did not do his homework; his parents did not carefully watch over his progress. And if the administration decides to forbid bad grades, then the teachers return to the tried and true method of writing a "3" [equivalent to the American grade of "D"] when a "2" ["F"] is meant. In this traditional teaching method the student quickly loses interest in education; and it is not surprising that, by the sixth or seventh grade, he or she is present in class only physically. Is it the child's fault?

In preparing a lesson using the alternative model, the specifics are entirely different. The teacher finds himself in the role of the student, carrying to term his understanding of the instructional content and in a position of self-growth. First, the teacher must creatively "package" the content. Second, he must plan for how the students are most likely to learn. In order to carry out these two tasks, the teacher must himself search for methods and standards, which is almost never done by the teacher-as-translator.

It is important to note that the strict control over instructional methods that was imposed in the 1970s and 1980s rooted out any attempt at creativity and turned the teacher into a worker at an educational conveyer belt, capable only of producing clones with the same ways of thinking and acting. Even if this system did occasionally produce extraordinary results, those results were achieved in spite of the system, not because of it.

An analysis from a nontraditional point of view of this traditional methodology also led us to understand the necessity of establishing a new administrative position. The first step was the attempt to work together with the teacher to plan changes (reforms) in the professional situation. It was obvious that this step could be effective only with a teacher who was already psychologically ready for change. New ways of teaching demanded a relatively unconstrained search for educational methods. This led to the necessity of interaction with colleagues from various regions of the country and participation in discussions and seminars. Teachers had to relearn how to teach. (At that time, the best place for this learning to take place was undoubtedly the Evrika Center for Socio-Educational Planning, founded by A.I. Adamskii, a famous comrade-in-arms of the editor of the *Uchitelskaya Gazeta* [Teachers' Gazette], A.F. Matveev.)

Then came the most difficult stage of the teachers' innovative work: the realization of an idealistic conception within the context of existing traditional methodology — in effect, programming and running an experiment. This experiment would not succeed without support and help from the administration, and the previous regime had driven out all similar experimentation. Thus arose the new professional administrative position that we called the socio-educational methodologist. The main task of this methodologist is the creation of experimental niches for innovating teachers.

The introduction of innovative teaching techniques also created other new tasks for the administration:

- analysis of the educational situation,
- planning its development,
- evaluating the planned model,
- programming the experimental realization of the model,
- closely supervising the experiment,
- evaluating the results, and
- constructively integrating the experiment with traditional educational methodology.

These new administrative challenges forced us not only to alter the demands of our administrative system, but also led to a bifurcation in the oversight and administration of the educational process. The problem was that it turned out to be physically and psychologically impossible to combine the new administrative duties with the traditional tasks. There was a large number of problems inherent in attempting to keep stable a system with very narrowly delimited educational methods. Innovative instructional methods could not easily fit into the existing education framework, especially since any innovative methods also worked to undermine tradition. (In other words, the tradition did not evolve, but approached catastrophe!) Therefore, the structure of the school administration had to change, as did the supervisory duties of the administrators.

From the very first, it became obvious that planning any kind of detailed ideal school model would seriously hinder the development of individual schools, because it would force all participants in the process to move along in one "ideal" direction, which could not possibly be perfect for any number of reasons. For example, we did not want to get too specific, because that would ruin the whole idea of letting teachers be creative with lesson plans. Thus a major concern for us was constructing a valid evaluation framework. The principle of individual development and evolution was more applicable to social activity, and the planned boundaries of the model were to stop at conceptual conditions of development. In this way, our model was limited by a set of fixed goals and the conditions under which they were to be realized.

At the next stage, when the innovative model was generally accepted and when we had divided the administrative functions, a new problem arose: the coordination of the traditional and innovative education institutions. We saw that few teachers were in situations where they could choose their own methods because many city schools did not yet work according to our model. Traditional teaching techniques "conserved," or preserved, the traditional methodological framework with the inevitable requirement of functional stability. On the other hand, innovative teaching techniques allowed for theoretical and practical creativity on the part of teachers, and our model provided socio-educational support for their efforts. Moreover, the experimental platform allowed for the testing of instructional methods and the development of new teaching methods. To coordinate these three elements, we introduced a support service focusing on methodology, expertise, and communication. In this way, our model completely solved the problem of integrating innovation and tradition and allowed for a cyclical development of the individual and of the general education framework.

Our innovative teaching institute was built on the principle of laboratories; in other words, it was centered on research and practical workshops. Among these was a group of laboratories for advanced and developmental education, early education and early childhood development, remedial education and family education, educational technologies, and play-based learning. The laboratory for socio-educational planning developed a program of specialization among students in the social work department of the youth institute. From 1992 onward, the complex, together with the institute, began to offer courses to students studying this field. The goal was to prepare planning specialists in innovative instructional methods.

Finally, to emphasize what I have said previously, it is important to note that the Ismailovo education complex was formed as a result of work done on the development of effective, creative instructional methods. It was born within a socio-educational complex that, in turn, was based on an analysis of the sociocultural situation in one of the districts of Moscow. In any planning job the subjective factor undoubtedly plays a large role; but nonetheless I wish to underscore that until all of the constituent parts of a developmental system of education appear in a large city such as Moscow, there is in its eastern part, in Ismailovo, a certain body of experience that can help others to avoid mistakes in a field that is new not so much because of its goals as by the methods in which they are achieved.

INNOVATIVE PROCESSES
IN RURAL SCHOOLS

G.F. Suvorova

Galina F. Suvorova is a doctor of pedagogic sciences and a professor at the Public School Institute of the Russian Academy of Education.

More than 40% of Russian students study in rural schools. For this reason, it is natural to wonder whether Russia's democratic reformation has reached into the provinces and, if so, what were the results, what did the farmer's child or the village teacher gain?

It is possible to assert with a certain degree of confidence that the democratization of Russian society has in fact reached the rural school, though not perhaps in all possible manifestations. The most obvious changes have been in external aspects, for example, in the organization of instruction during any given week and in the duration of the school day.

The tiring sameness of the six-day school week and the 45-minute class period have been replaced by a spectrum of options, allowing each school to determine the optimal conditions for learning. For example, when flexibility was allowed, some rural schools immediately shifted to a five-day school week. But even with the five-day schedule, there were significant variations. Some schools made Wednesday a day off, others Saturday, depending on the desires of the children and the needs of the parents.

Even with the six-day week, there are some "light" days. More often than not, a light day is Wednesday or Thursday, the days when students are most worn out. On these days, the school schedule is built around art, physical education, and shop classes, providing an antidote to a heavy academic schedule on the other days.

Each school also uses "free" days differently, some for supplementary in-school activities, others for field trips, library work, and enrichment and remedial classes.

This variety also extends to the length of a class period in the rural school. Class length ranges from 35 minutes in the primary grades to 50 minutes for the upper classes. Time freed up during the school day is put to use as a "health period" for active games outside, for five-minute exercise breaks during classes, for enrichment programs and clubs, or for other extracurricular academic activities. Enrichment and extracurriculars are especially common in schools that draw their student body from a number of different villages, as it is difficult to get students together outside of school for special projects.

During the past three years rural schools have begun experimenting with "immersion" in some subjects. At first, this touched only one-hour and two-hour subjects. For example, instead of studying biology or geography once or twice a week, the material is taught in one large block, with students spending an hour or two hours daily with a given subject. As a result, the subject is covered in half the time it would take ordinarily, and the quality of the knowledge base and skills that are acquired is positively affected.

Some schools also have turned away from the traditional quarter-based academic year and have replaced it with two or three semesters.

These kinds of changes represent the character of the organizational reforms that have taken place in rural schools. The educational consequences of these changes have not yet been studied. But the process itself, in which schools seek out new approaches to the organization of the school calendar, year, week, day, and class period, is a positive step forward and reflects the willingness of rural teachers and administrators to leave behind the decades-old conservative tradition and to look ahead to experimentation and new possibilities.

Because the educational process is an integrated whole, the reforms affect the curricular content of the rural schools as well. One of the most radical reforms is the creation of local curricula. The democratic reforms in the Russian school system have allowed each school to develop its own individual curriculum, based on a basic educational plan. Of course, the best rural schools have created and continue to create curricula and to select those academic disciplines that reflect the education that the teachers feel is best for the students of their particular school.

For example, it is now typical to find foreign language taught in primary schools, whereas previously this was not the case. Previously, the foreign language instruction was different for each school. In some schools, foreign languages were offered as supplementary 20-minute classes at the close of the school day. In others, the classes were a regular part of the daily class schedule. In some schools, foreign language instruction started in first grade; in others, in second or fourth grade.

It is understandable that teachers want to offer their students the broadest possible education. However, many rural schools did not offer foreign language instruction at all, because parents were unfamiliar with any foreign language or because of a shortage of foreign language instructors for rural schools. Foreign language instruction has benefits for an entire village when its students can eagerly exclaim: "We're studying English (German, French)!" In all cases, for students with language abilities, the foreign language is a positive benefit. And, of course, interest in a foreign language is something about which both students and their parents can be proud.

Rhythmic gymnastics is another subject that is popular in rural schools. It is a synthesis of physical education (specifically gymnastics) and dance (principally folk dance and ballroom dance). Even though this subject matter is somewhat undefined and is usually taught by primary school teachers or, in the best case, by physical education teachers, it is still useful, especially for the shy, awkward rural child.

A more important reform, in my opinion, is the greater emphasis placed on traditions and customs of the people of a given area. The new subject — social studies (which may be called "History of Our Region," "Our People," "Folklore," etc.) — can be found more and more frequently in the curricula of rural schools. This subject, as a rule, integrates the study of history, geography, ethnology, literature, music, and ethnography. Social studies is an open road, where teachers can design their own courses according to their interests and capacities.

In some cases, the social studies curriculum features descriptions of customs of Russians and other peoples who live in Russia, of their daily lives, their work, their arts and crafts. In other cases, it features examples of folk creativity: stories, tall tales, songs, counting rhymes, and national costumes. Sometimes the instruction is largely verbal. In other situations students learn through hands-on experiences by producing objects in the folk style. The most successful programs include elements of both approaches. In primary grades, students learn basic information about folk games, customs, and the holidays of their region and village. The children participate in holiday events and games. Later, the course includes information about the local people and their character, about local saints, heroes, and leaders. In the upper classes the course introduces students to the fundamentals of the local philosophy and the spiritual values of the local people. With the great number of possible variations, with all their "rawness," such courses allow students to learn about national traditions and to preserve them.*

A related issue involves the development of a regional component for courses of history, geography, and literature. Take, for example, literature. The canon of Russian classical literature is vast and simply cannot be squeezed into the framework of the basic school literature curriculum. Many great works are only mentioned, and there are some that students never even become aware of. Including a regional and local component into the literature curriculum broadens the knowledge base of the students and familiarizes them with local authors and poets. For example, the course, "Literature of the Russian North," includes poems by N. Klyuev (who is mentioned only briefly and only in connection with S. Esenin in the standard curriculum), N. Rubtsov (who is not mentioned at all), and excerpts from the manuscripts, speeches, tales, and other works by V. Belov. In this way, rural students become acquainted with an entire field of literature, which raises their cultural level yet another notch.

---

*Translator's note: During the Soviet period, there was an official policy of assimilation. The many non-Russian peoples of that era were encouraged to learn Russian and to give up their native customs and traditions.

Reforms also have affected teaching methods. Rural teachers, while not completely discarding traditional teaching techniques, enrich their teaching by using research-based innovative methods. For example, the subjects of biology and chemistry are highly relevant to the rural student. Smaller classes allow teachers to replace lectures and demonstrations with hands-on experiments, which allow the students to practice their theoretical knowledge and apply their skills toward agricultural ends. Rural students from an early age are involved in the work of the farm, and the knowledge and skills of managing an agricultural enterprise are vitally important to them.

The use of games as educational tools already has received wide acceptance among rural teachers and, in fact, has become part of the standard teaching methodology. Teachers carefully prepare role-playing, imitational, and organizational games; and the effectiveness of these methods has naturally increased. The fad has been subsumed by goal-oriented methodology.

This year some experimental rural schools have received examples of the newest technology. Educators developed the first literary classes based on the hypertext technology. For the first time ever, literary compositions will be studied while not "following the author" in a strict linear manner. Hypertext allows students to follow any number of thematic connections and chains of meaning. Thus students will focus not only on what the "author tried to say" but on what, in effect, was actually stated in the text. New methods of deconstructing texts and of following connections between different texts are beginning to appear. In order to introduce the new technology to rural schools, we have the hypertext based on the well-known material by A.S. Pushkin: the story, "The Station Watcher," as well as key character development scenes from *Evgeny Onegin*. Students absorb the material through a non-linear text, wherein the structural elements consist of the standard linear pieces. The non-linearity of the text means that after reading a certain segment, the text bifurcates; and students can choose from a number of further reading options. In other words, the technology allows for realistic conditions of individualized learning. I expect that the new techniques of working with the written text are a major breakthrough into qualitatively new methods of teaching and learning.

Of course, in describing these innovations, I have focused on the examples that characterize the activities of large numbers of schools. It is possible to get the impression that Russian rural schools have no unresolved problems. Obviously, this is not the case. There are, in fact, many very serious problems.

First of all is the crumbling infrastructure. Up to 7% of all school buildings do not meet basic safety standards, and more than a quarter of all schools need major repairs. Many schools also are ill-supplied with audiovisual equipment, visual aids, and similar materials. Educational technology that the schools received in the 1970s and 1980s has, for the most part, worn out; and new technology cannot be acquired because it is very expensive. The situation with textbooks is even more critical. Even though there is adequate variety in available textbooks, the print runs are insufficient to supply all students with the needed books. Finally, not all families, especially those with many children, can afford even notebooks.

Because many schools lack teachers, not all subjects are taught in all schools. There also is a shortage of fuel, forcing many schools to drop school bus routes. Many students have to walk miles to get to school every day. There are similar difficulties with vocational education in the upper grades. A lack of transport and on-campus housing and small class sizes means that not all schools are able to create vocational education programs.

There are other problems as well. But the rural school is still alive and is in search of new productive educational methods, methods that answer the needs of the 21st century.

THE REBIRTH OF NATIONAL TRADITIONS
N.V. Prokhina

N.V. Prokhina has enjoyed decorative painting on wood since her childhood. During the last four years, she has been working at a school with a special intensive study program of the display arts. This program was developed jointly with Honored Teacher of Russia F.P. Kuzmina. The program's goal is to develop the artistic abilities of the students. The history of creativity and traditions of folk arts and crafts hold a special place in this program.

The idea of familiarizing children with the Russian national culture as part of the renaissance of Russian folk art traditions arose in our school a long time ago.

We are grateful to award-winning teacher Faina Petrovna Kuzmina for putting these ideas into practice and creating a school with an intensive expressive arts study program. She is an architect by training who felt a calling to become a teacher. The school she founded was unusual in that children begin to study art from the very earliest ages. In order to identify the children's talents, a preschool *gymnasium** was organized for children as young as four years. The gymnasium teachers not only prepare students to enter the first grade but also develop their artistic abilities. After attending the gymnasium, students take a drawing exam. The result of the exam, in combination with interviews, is used to place the students in the first grade.

The educational goal of this school is to identify the most gifted and talented youngsters and to offer them an education that transcends the mandatory minimum while allowing them to choose supplementary subjects for intensive study. The art course is taught in two parallel parts: the academic study of drawing and painting and the study of Russian folk art traditions. In this way, we teach students about art as a part of the world culture while accenting the most important aspects of the Russian artistic tradition: folk art, handicrafts, dances, songs, poetry, and theater.

To this day, the study of the Russian decorative and practical crafts is the domain of kindergartens and the primary grades,

Gymnasium, in this sense, means a school focused on a particular subject or set of subjects, in this case, traditional arts.

because the folk arts are close to children's art: spontaneous, unforced, directly expressive, natural, and simple.

In our school the Russian national art curriculum is divided into three levels: 1) first through fourth grades, 2) fifth through ninth grades, and 3) tenth through eleventh grades.

Level 1. The first level of art education consists of a single system of drawing, painting, and folk art classes. A detailed investigation is made into the individual characteristics of each child, his or her skills and abilities. Then the child is provided with experiences and instruction so that, by the end of fourth grade, the child is able to determine his or her further interests independently.

Level 2. At the second level, the study of Russian national art becomes more intensive, with the student learning about its history, traditions, masters, and modern art forms. The student is able to study seriously basic kinds of Russian decorative and practical crafts and to develop skills needed to work with different kinds of materials (wood, paint, clay, fabric). At this level, the curriculum is organized to meet the following goals. Students will:

- Study Russian folk art and become familiar with the history, everyday life, and art of people;
- Develop curiosity and observation skills;
- Develop wood-painting, molding, and toy-painting skills;
- Study folk decorative patterns and painting traditions, developing original compositions based on the study of originals, copying examples, mastering painting skills, color palettes, and specific painting techniques;
- Complete practical assignments;
- Prepare to choose a profession connected to folk arts and crafts or enter an arts academy; and
- Participate in mandatory field trips to museums and exhibitions featuring Russian artworks.

However, unlike many other schools and institutes, our school has a truly invaluable treasure — a museum of utilitarian folk arts and crafts. The collection was acquired one "grain" at a time by F.P. Kuzmina, a teacher, and by her students and their parents.

The collection contains more than 1,500 pieces that reflect folk traditions and the life of a Russian village. There are furnishings from a traditional Russian log cabin, a large collection of samovars, antique irons, spinning wheels, and toys from all different corners of Russia. It is important to note that this is not simply a museum, but a *working* museum. All items are used as teaching tools during class lessons. Children not only can look at and touch these objects, but also can copy them in their work.

Theoretical lectures and conversations are held within the walls of the museum. Even the classroom in which children first learn about traditional folk arts is an unusual one. It is decorated by objects created by the students themselves, and the desks and chairs are arranged not in rows, but in such a way that the students sit facing one another, so that each can see what his neighbor is doing.

There are many flowers in the classroom, for flowers are absolutely necessary. Russian craftsmen looked to nature to give beauty to their decorative paintings. It is difficult to create rural conditions in an urban setting, but house plants can help a lot. In taking care of the flowers and in observing them closely, students can more easily reproduce nature's beauty in their artwork. There also is a collection of dried flowers and leaves in the classroom, which is frequently put to use.

What traditional styles do the students study in the folk art program? Following are some examples:

- Decorative painting on wood according to the traditions of Gododets, Khokhloma, Polkhovski, Maidan, Krutets, Prikamye, Permogorye, Mezen, and Rakula.
- Decorative painting on metal in the traditions of Zhoskov and Nizhni (Lower) Tagil.
- Decorative painting on ceramics in the traditions of *majolica* painting, Gzhel, and Rostov *finifit* painting.*

---

*These well-known styles in Russia are simply referred to as "ceramics" in the United States.

- Decorative painting on papier-mâché from Palekh, Kholui, Metera, and Fedoskino.
- Making and painting clay toys in the traditions of Kargopol, Zhbannikovsk, Khludnevsk, Ryazan, Filimonov, Dymkovsk, and Torzhok toy craftsmen.
- Scarves and shawls.
- Lace making from Vologda, Eletsk, Balakhna, and Razyan.
- Weaving.
- Embroidery.
- Russian folk dress.

Special attention is paid to decorative painting on wood and making and painting clay toys because of the availability of the necessary materials. Lace making, embroidery, and weaving are taught only theoretically, through a discussion, lecture, and demonstration of the subject. The applied part of the lesson consists of creating patterns and designs for each craft type.

Varnish-covered miniatures or decorative painting on papier-mâché are studied only theoretically because of the complexity of the production and painting techniques.

The study of Russian folk costumes is divided into stages. The beginning grades learn about sewing techniques and the traditional Russian seam stitches with which the clothes were made. In middle school, students learn about the principles of Russian folk dress production and the use of lace, weaving, and embroidery in its decoration. On the basis of these lessons, the students produce a pattern. Then, using the pattern, they sew cloth dolls, just as their great-grandmothers once did.

It is important to note that the students, while studying traditional crafts, learn not only about decorative painting and working with clay, but also about the traditions of Russian culture, habits and customs of those times when these crafts were born, and about the master craftsmen of modern and ancient times. Each craft, after all, is a separate, vivid page in the book of our history and culture. Therefore, every subject is built roughly around a model that begins with discussion of folk arts and crafts.

The students study historical background, how the craft arose, traditions, techniques, designs, and master craftsmen. Teachers demonstrate and lead the students to examine samples from the school museum and to look through books, visual aids, and reproductions. Next, the students study specific techniques and practice elements, such as decorative painting. Then they create a composition, which may be a painting, a lace design, or a toy.

This model allows the student to gain a base of knowledge and skills in each type of folk craft and to study decorative painting, starting with the simple and ending with the very difficult. Each year, according to the skills already acquired, the students create objects beginning with those of the easiest designs and progressing to complicated compositions. We value most the qualities of thoroughness, dedication, and patience, which we try to get our students to develop. Only a knowledge of the roots of the craft and its artistic development can produce original craftsmen whose products will stand out from the great mass of goods produced today. The main goal of the study of practical decorative crafts, therefore, lies in developing the unique abilities of each student. Creativity is not duplication, but fantasy, the play of ideas, inventiveness.

Folk crafts, like any other art form, are purely a creative endeavor. But since the educational process takes place in a school setting, it is necessary to evaluate this creativity. How is this possible? No matter how well or badly a child draws, each picture is his expression, his art.

The task of evaluation is made somewhat easier by the fact that the students studying in our school are those who have always loved to draw and who, from their very first school years, have been studying the visual arts. But no matter what standards have been set in each painting style, every student has his own perception of the surrounding world. In his "art" the student expresses the knowledge that he has acquired and processed.

Considering the special circumstances of each separate learning process and the individual abilities of each student, we must evaluate every single kind of school assignment. There are practice exercises, in which the student is required to demonstrate certain skills and show that he or she is making an effort. In this case, the student is graded on performance. It is more difficult to evaluate creative work. This evaluation must be approached from two points of view: first, the amount of effort expended and the skills demonstrated, as above, and second, creativity in producing the composition and choosing colors and respect for tradition combined with individual artistic vision.

The products of folk craftsmanship have always served a household function; but more than that, they also bring joy to the eye. Kind and able hands always produce kind and beautiful objects, which also please others. That is why craftsmen gave away their best work to their close friends and loved ones. This tradition is alive to this day. How wonderful it is to see students painstakingly bend over a simple kitchen cutting board, putting down the color one brush stroke at a time. After all, each object is not simply a class assignment, but a present already slated to be given to someone.

At our school, students also can sell their artwork. From ancient times, folk craftsmen produced goods for the market. The better and more beautiful a product, the quicker it could be sold — and the more money it would bring. In the early grades, students do not yet possess the necessary skills and abilities to make work for sale, but their desire to draw has no bounds. All of their work is dedicated in advance to people close to them. In the upper grades, students are trying to earn money and paint with an eye to the market. In this case, as a rule, they are thinking less of the art and more about their future earnings.

In conclusion, we would like to mention yet another Russian tradition that has been revived in our school. Springtime across Russia has been a traditional time for local fairs, to which artisans travel to sell their work. Each spring, we also hold such a fair. The participants include the teachers and the students, who demonstrate their craftsmanship, skills, and abilities and show off their creativity. The fair is a continuation of the Russian folk art tradition. These are unique displays of the work done through the year.

FROM COMPUTER LITERACY
TO LOGICAL THOUGHT

A.A. Muranov

A.A. Muranov is a graduate of the Mathematics Department of the Moscow Pedagogic University and taught physics, mathematics, and information science for 12 years. He currently is the director of the Center for Informational and Educational Technologies and is working on resolving problems surrounding the integrated approach to education.

The everyday use of computing machines and data-based technologies in the developed countries did not make every person a programmer, just as the popularization of television did not make each viewer a television repairman or a television journalist. However, in the same way that all educated persons receive a basic understanding of the principles by which televisions operate in their physics classes, so do they need to acquire a general knowledge of the principles underlying personal computer and informational technologies. This knowledge should extend their understanding of basic programming and familiarity with the most common software.

Personal computer users can be divided, rather arbitrarily, into 1) software users, 2) software users who also write simple programs for their own use, and 3) programmers who write software for the use of others.

Most people who use the computer fall into the first category. Thus schools do not need to train each student to be a programmer. However, a basic computer class (10th or 11th grade) usually is tilted toward the programming side, in that students learn algorithms and a programming language. This class may be unnecessary for the first type of computer user; it comes too late for the second and third types of user. Our experience with this type of study shows that it is inadequate for the following reasons:

- This type of program does not allow for the unique educational needs and interests of the students.
- A late start using the computer does not allow us to develop the subject to its fullest potential.
- The course is not integrated with other school subjects.

The algorithm-based thinking skills that are in some form necessary to all students should, as a rule, be taught earlier than the 10th or 11th grade, because children's thinking styles are for the most part formed in primary school. The late start to such learning, as well as the bias toward programming skills, are the major deficiencies of the standard curriculum.

Also, our experience in teaching these courses has shown a great deal of variation in students' abilities and in their needs. From this perspective, it is impossible to solve all problems in teaching computers within the framework of one course. Instead, it is necessary to create a system of teaching computers and integrating them into the learning process. Such a system was developed in the Ismailovo educational complex through the Center for Informational and Educational Technologies (CIET).

In creating this system, our primary concern was that, given the high cost of the technology, the computers should be used to the fullest extent possible. In the educational process, use of the personal computer (PC) is not only a subject to be taught. The computer is also an educational tool, or medium. And any medium is beneficial only when it is used properly. Therefore, our most interesting task, but also the most difficult from the methodological and practical points of view, was developing ways to use the computers and information technologies in teaching various subjects.

In order to fully realize the potential of the personal computers, the following conditions were necessary: 1) an early familiarity of the students with the PC as a tool, 2) the existence of adequate software and the means to acquire and put it to use, 3) teachers who are interested in using information technologies in their work and who are able to adapt their teaching methods to include them, 4) the readiness of computer teachers to work together with teachers of other subjects and to train them to use the new technologies, and 5) a comprehensive system for introducing the new technologies.

In creating a system of teaching computing basics and using computers in the educational process, we held the following statements as givens:

- Computers in schools are simultaneously objects to be studied and a learning medium.
- The "computer" is not an educational goal in itself, but rather supplements collective and individual research under a number of didactic forms and teaching methods.
- The goal of teaching computer science is to instill an operational thinking style.
- The content of computer education must be differentiated, based on the abilities and interests of the students, while still providing the fundamental skills and concepts.
- Students should start learning about computers in an organized fashion in primary school (3rd to 5th grades), because thinking styles are formed, for the most part, in this age group.
- Separate groups of interested and capable students should be able to study programming as a vocational subject (8th- to 11th-grade mathematics classes) as well as in special-interest clubs and in a departmental class.
- The use of computers in the learning process by the teacher, individual students, or groups of students could significantly increase the effectiveness of the lessons.
- The computer lab should be available to students outside of class hours and during special periods.
- Computer use should be planned in such a way that students steadily increase their abilities to work independently at the PC and build investigative and creative skills.
- Computers should offer the school an entire toolbox of educational techniques for a variety of subjects.
- For the majority of students in the upper classes, the computer should become a passive but necessary aid throughout the educational process.
- High school students should be able to participate in productive work that involves computers.

Computer science classes and the computerization of the school as a whole should be part of a system that teaches fundamental concepts and skills to each student, allows each student the flexibility to study the aspect of computer science that is most relevant, and fully takes advantage of the possibilities generated by the presence of the computers and the software in the school.

In the system developed and tested at the CIET of the Ismail-ovo school, the most interesting facet is the integrated approach to school subjects. In this approach, the Computer Science class is organized according to "frame" and "block" principles. This basic organization of the subject is a data-based way of looking at the world, in which any process or event can be seen in terms of data preservation, manipulation, or transmission. This is a very wide framework that can encompass practically any content that is needed for a given age or a given group of children. The three basic blocks are:

Logical Culture (the culture of thought): learning by means of processing information. This block includes the acquisition of algorithmic, abstract, logical, intuitive, and creative thinking skills and methods of organizing the thinking process.

Information Culture: learning by means of seeking information. In this block, students learn to work with sources of information, to classify information, and to determine the meaning of the information accumulated by mankind.

Assistance in studying various subjects. In this block, students acquire knowledge and skills in various subject areas taught at the school while simultaneously gathering materials for the first and second blocks.

The diagram on page 69 shows how these blocks and frames are distributed.

Since the system of teaching computers and using them for teaching specific subjects was developed five years ago, it has been continuously tested in our complex and has produced positive results. This system has allowed us to use computer lessons to develop the logical thinking skills and creative abilities of our students in parallel with teaching them to use computers as early as the third grade. Most valuable are the Thinking and Computer

Level	Experimental Classes		Compensatory/ Supplemental	Basic Program		Additional Components/ Special Interest
	Basic (CEIT)	Special		Mandatory	Intensive	
1	Integrated study and development of logical thinking skills using information technology and educational software. Students learn basic computer theory and user skills. (3 hours/week)					
2(1-3)		Introduction to the computer: computer theory, logical thinking skills, problem solving, and user skills. Thinking curriculum. (2 hours/week)				
3(1-4)				Introduction to the computer: computer theory, logical thinking skills, problem solving, and user skills. Thinking curriculum. (2 hours/week)		
3(1-3)			Use of computers to develop thinking skills, fine motor skills, and to practice material taught in other classes. (1 hour/week)			
4(1-4)						
5	Computer lessons oriented to material in general education curriculum. Use of information technologies in independent study. (2 hours/week)					
6	Computer classes centered on material taught in general education classes. (2 hours/week)	Computer classes centered on material taught in general education classes. (1 hour/week)		Computer classes centered on material taught in general education classes. (1 hour/week)	Departmental course: Learning to Program. (2 hours/week)	System of themed clubs.
7						
8	Information technologies and elements of programming with consideration of students' majors. (2 hours/week)	Information technologies and elements of programming with consideration of students' majors. (2 hours/week)		Information technologies and elements of programming with consideration of students' majors. (2 hours/week)		
9					Programming and specific elements of mathematics within the context of the mathematics curriculum. Independent computer use. (4 hours/week)	Special classes in various fields of computer science.
10						
11	Independent computer use in computer lab.	Independent computer use in computer lab.		Independent computer use in computer lab.		

Class curricula, which I discuss later. However, we would like to better use the integrative possibilities of computers.

During the second stage of our work, we formed experimental classes in the primary grades in which the curriculum was built around the principles of information science. The basis for the integration was concepts that were common to all subjects, such as quantity, description, classification, correspondence, dependence, and proof (described in simple terms for the youngest children). This curriculum assumes that there is agreement about the definition and application of these concepts. The fact that teachers are aware of the universality of these concepts and their use in various subjects helps the students to better understand them and to learn to use them starting in the earliest grades. The integrated approach based on these key concepts also allows students to assimilate course material more quickly, and the resulting "extra" time is used to teach students to apply the new knowledge to concrete situations.

This curriculum also assumes that education means, first of all, that students are taught how to know and how to ponder questions they themselves have asked and then how to proceed to a logically correct analysis of their answers to these questions. This work cannot be done with one separate subject but must be built into all the learning that the children do. The solution lies not in the planning of any individual course, but in the right organization of all subjects — and not so much in terms of the content, but in the teaching techniques to be used.

Reading, writing, and mathematics curricula in these grades are built on the base of the existing grades 1 through 3 curricula with the introduction of the integration and elements of developmental education.

The curriculum assumes the introduction of computer lessons as aids to learning the basic subjects of any given educational cycle. These lessons also help students develop their logical thinking skills. The lesson plans are developed in-house by the primary school and computer science teachers of our complex.

In conclusion, following are two curriculum examples: the Thinking curriculum and the Computer Class curriculum.

Thinking Curriculum

This curriculum is developed in grades 4 and 5.

Goals:
1. To use the PC as a means of teaching students various school subjects.
2. To familiarize students with using the PC and software.
3. To teach students to think algorithmically and operationally, and to teach educational programming languages.
4. To develop creative and logical thinking skills.

Methods:

The Thinking course curriculum was developed for students in the general primary school classes. Ideally, the computer teachers and the primary classroom teachers work together creatively in teaching this course. This course is the part of the school curriculum that unites information science, the content of the other school subjects, and the development of the logical thinking skills of the students. The basic unit of the course is one class lesson combined with one creative assignment. Each of these units is built around several organizational principles:

- The basic constituent blocks are covered in parallel;
- The students participate in various activities;
- The course is integrated in content with other school subjects; and
- The course performs a service function for other subjects.

Students use set theory, solve problems, manipulate data, seek information using various media, and develop creativity, among other activities. Lesson themes for the first year include:

- Using the computer in everyday life to provide for safety (1 hour).
- The concept of data and types of data (2 hours).
- Informational processes (3 hours).
- Command languages (2 hours).
- Algorithms (4 hours).

- Structure of the computer (1 hour).
- Coordinate system (3 hours).
- Flow problems (2 hours).
- Working with data (6 hours).
- Computers and school subjects (4 hours).
- Problem solving (1 hour).

In the second year, some of the lessons and time lengths include:

- Algorithms and programs (7 hours).
- Complex algorithms (6 hours).
- Plans and structures (6 hours).
- Communications (3 hours).
- Algorithms, command languages, models (4 hours).
- Using the computer to do work (6 hours).

At the same time that students use the computer for assignments, they also work on creative projects using the computer and work with different types of software and educational programs. The actual results of this curriculum depend on the available technology, software, and the abilities of the teachers who implement the curriculum.

Computer Class Curriculum

This curriculum is most developed in grades 6 and 7.

Goals:
1. To use the computer as a means to learn the various subjects of the general school curriculum.
2. To practice further computer skills and to become more familiar with computer software.
3. To master operational thinking skills while studying computer programming languages.
4. To develop creative and logical thinking abilities.

Methods:
The Computer Class curriculum is designed for those youngsters who have studied the Thinking curriculum in the fourth and

fifth grades. In this course, information science and computers are used as a means of teaching other school subjects for 65% to 70% of the time. The goals of the course are met by having students work with software applications that incorporate the content of the school subjects. The lessons that deal with learning certain concepts or skills directly connected to information science or computers will be presented in terms of learning, practicing, or being tested in some school subject. Most of the class time of the course will be spent developing the students' logical thinking skills.

Those students interested in more intensive study of information science and computer programming can participate in a parallel class (departmental class) with a special curriculum. In addition, students also can choose to participate in clubs that deal with specific aspects of computers: computer graphics, logic games, turtle graphics, desktop publishing, and others.

The actual results of the course depend on the available technology and software. Course contents includes:

1. Geometric figures and the LOGO programming language. Subject: mathematics.

Concepts and skills: Angles, degree measurements of angles, angles of more than 180 degrees, the sum of the angles in a triangle and polygons, equilateral polygons and their properties, symmetry, and the coordinate system.

Information science: Understanding procedures, variables, parameters, and recursion.

Creativity: Developing artistic abilities while building geometric designs, working on creative assignments.

Lesson content: Students write LOGO programs to draw various geometric figures, learn the relationship between the figures and the angles within them, and carry out experiments in building geometric figures by varying parameters to determine general laws, which they later prove using geometry theorems.

2. Text processing on the computer. Subjects: Russian, literature, English.

Concepts and skills: As determined by Russian and English language teachers.

Information science: Familiarly with word processing software, keyboarding skills.

Creativity: Writing and editing short stories, developing language skills.

Lesson content: Students practice entering Russian or English texts that are later compared to an original already in the computer, editing prepared texts that are missing parts, typing dictated texts (computer dictation), and writing new texts on various themes, which are later included in a published journal.

3. Saving and processing information in a data base. Subjects: history, geography, library science.

Concepts and skills: As determined by history and geography teachers.

Information science: Familiarity with database management software, methods of storing information in a database and later manipulating this information to achieve certain goals.

Creativity: A creative approach to the selection of data for systemization and the analysis of systematized data depending on the school subject, which determines the data that is used.

Lesson content: Students learn to process data in a prepared database with the goal of reaching conclusions based on questions asked by the teacher, adding additional information to the database, and correcting information.

4. Using the computer to automate different types of work. Subjects: mathematics, physics, art, shop.

Concepts and skills: As determined by the subject teachers.

Information science: Familiarity with relevant software, the concept of a command language, the command language system, working in a command language environment, and writing algorithms in the command language.

Creativity: Developing creative abilities and skills in choosing methods to solve a given problem.

Lesson content: Students work with software that automates the work of an artist (a graphics processor), the researcher (physics and mathematics modeling programs, electronic tables), operator of machine tools with computerized numerical control, computer-aided designer, etc.

5. Creating algorithms. Subjects: mathematics, natural science subjects.

Concepts and skills: Structured thinking, the ability to plan a solution to a problem in exact detail.

Information science: The concept of a command language, the command language system, working in a command language environment, writing algorithms in the command language, understanding the structure approach to the creation of algorithms.

Creativity: A creative approach to determining the methods by which a problem is solved, differentiating between the general and the special cases.

Lesson content: Students write programs in various command languages in Russian-language programming systems and create algorithms to solve problems for specific subject areas (mathematics, physics, everyday problems, etc.).

6. Educational and testing programs. Subjects: all subjects, on a case-by-case basis.

Concepts and skills: As determined by the subject teacher, given the constraints of the available software.

Information science: Familiarity with relevant software, keyboarding skills.

Creativity: As determined by the available software.

Lesson content: Students work with given testing or drilling or educational programs individually and in groups.

7. Information and measurement. Subject: information science.

Concepts and skills: Types of data, measuring the quantity of data, coding data, inputting data into the computer.

Lesson content: Theoretical study of the material and work with educational software.

8. The computer operating system. Subject: information science.

Concepts and skills: Learning about operating systems and

computer file structures, developing the skills needed for practical work on the computer.

Lesson content: Students learn about the operating system of a given computer and develop the skills needed to use it.

9. What a computer can and cannot do, setting up tasks for the computer. Subjects: all school subjects.

Concepts and skills: Understanding when a computer can help solve a problem and when it cannot and developing the skills to formulate a statement of the problem so that it can be solved by the computer.

Lesson content: Theoretical discussion of the problem, describing the problem so that it can be solved on the computer, using the computer to solve the problem.